Published 2014. Centum Books Ltd.
Unit 1, Upside Station Building Solsbro Road,
Torquay, Devon, UK, TQ26FD

books@centumbooksltd.co.uk

Front cover photography – David Venni

£7.99

CONTENTS

OODLES OF OLLY

SCHOOL DAYS...
Olly attended Notley High School in Braintree, Essex. He still sponsors the school football side.

OH BABY!
Olly absolutely adores his nephew Louie (his sister's son). He even has a photo of him on his earpiece, while performing.

Fact File

NAME: Oliver Stanley Murs

D.O.B.   14/05/84

HEIGHT: 1.76m

EYE COLOUR: Blue

HAIR COLOUR: Light Brown

STAR SIGN: Taurus

HOME TOWN: Witham, Essex

FAMILY: Parents, Vicky-Lynn & Peter
                   Murs. Sister, Fay. Twin
                   brother, Ben.

FAVOURITE FOOD: Chicken

HOBBIES: Football, Video Games, Films/
                   TV Series, Collecting Bobbleheads,
                   Golf (Early Days!).

Here To

It's hard to believe it's been five whole years since a nervous lad from Essex haltingly took to the stage in front of the judging panel on a TV programme called The X Factor. Back then he was just a working class guy with a dream, but fast-forward to 2015 and Olly Murs is a global superstar. A critically acclaimed and widely adored singer-songwriter, he is now on his forth album, has had 4 UK number 1's and countless hits under his belt - plus a presenting career to boot. But where did it all begin?

Unbelievably, had Olly not suffered a tear to the cruciate ligament in his knee he might have come to our attention in a totally different field — football. A gifted player, Olly played semi pro for his local team Witham Town FC, making it to the first team when the devastating injury squashed his ambitions of playing in the Premier League. Luckily, talented Olly had more than one string to his bow.

Olly grew up crooning along to Stevie Wonder and James Brown tracks in front of the mirror. With

STAY

a great-aunt who had performed in the West End and a great-great gran who'd been a famous trapeze artist, it was perhaps not surprising that Olly inherited more than a touch of their showmanship. A born performer, he'd sing at family parties and an impromptu karaoke session at his local pub quickly led to regular gigs. He even formed a band called the Small Town Blaggers with his friend John.

However, it was his bold decision to audition for The X Factor in 2009 that would ultimately change his life and give him the perfect platform to showcase his natural talent and fabulous charm. His future in the music industry seemed assured from the moment he received a standing ovation and Simon Cowell pronounced him "very, very, very cool." And so it has proved.

Since landing a deal with Epic and Syco post The X Factor, Olly's career has gone stratospheric. The killer combination of his voice, style, charisma and work ethic, so evident from the beginning, continues to impress those within the industry and ensure that his Murs Army of devoted fans keeps on growing. It looks like everyone's favourite Essex boy is here to stay.

Out And About With Olly

Olly's packed so much in to the last year it's been tough to keep track of him. While he's been out and about he's been running into all sorts of people. Take a peek inside Olly's personal photo album and see if you recognize any of the faces in his special selfies.

Bumping into Ashton Kutcher on a flight.

Me & Chezza at my management's summer party.

Me with JT!

Me & Robbie Monkey Business.

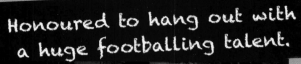
Honoured to hang out with a huge footballing talent.

Finally got to get up close and personal with José aka 'The Special One.'

Meeting one of my all-time heroes...

Bumped into the Modfather at The Royal Albert Hall!

... And another!

Family selfie with my favourite people!

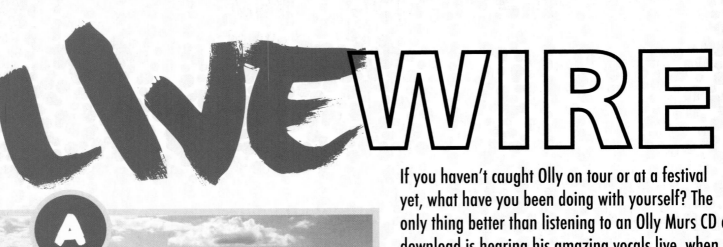

LIVE WIRE

If you haven't caught Olly on tour or at a festival yet, what have you been doing with yourself? The only thing better than listening to an Olly Murs CD or download is hearing his amazing vocals live, when you're practically sharing air with the great man. Check out the shots below and see if you can match them to the gig he was playing at the time.

A

B

C

E

D

1. GUILFEST, GUILDFORD

2. ODYSSEY ARENA, BELFAST

3. V FESTIVAL, CHELMSFORD

4. ROBBIE WILLIAMS 'TAKE THE CROWN' TOUR

5. iTUNES FESTIVAL

Olly IN THE STUDIO

Olly's been busy in the studio this year. He has been creating incredible new material for his fourth album and collaborating with some immensely talented writers and producers. We can't wait to finally hear the results of all his hard work, but for now we'll have to make do with some fun visuals from the man himself, which show exactly what he's been up to.

Olly's been recording at Abbey Road, the celebrated studios made famous by The Beatles album of the same name.

Is he working with dream team Guy Chambers and Robbie Williams or are they just hanging out? We'll have to wait and see.

...s been mastering crazy ...king instruments in a studio in ...thamptonshire.

With songwriter and producer Jamie Scott, who has written for One Direction and Little Mix.

The legend that is Mister Claude Kelly is evidently on board for album number four. Olly tweeted "Im in the studio with the real GARFIELD today@ClaudeKelly #Nevertrustasmilingcat."

Ed Drewett and Olly have resumed their writing collaboration. Ed and Olly previously penned smash-hit 'Dear Darlin' together.

We know he's been spotted in the studio with Preston from The Ordinary Boys!

NOW WE'RE REALLY EXCITED!

Tunes!

Part of Olly's huge appeal is his ability to write a cracking pop song. With the exception of 'What a Buzz', talented Olly co-wrote every track on his latest album 'Right Place Right Time'. He also co-penned three of his four number ones.

THE SINGLES

Dance With Me Tonight
Released 18th November 2011
Peak Chart Position - #1

Heart Skips A Beat (featuring Rizzle Kicks)
Released 19th August 2011
Peak Chart Position - #1

Troublemaker (featuring Flo Rida)
Released 16th November 2012
Peak Chart Position - #1

Please Don't Let Me Go
Released 27th August 2010
Peak Chart Position - #1

Thinking Of Me
Released 19th November 2010
Peak Chart Position - #4

Dear Darlin'
Released 24th May 2013
Peak Chart Position - #5

Army Of Two
Released 22nd March 2013
Peak Chart Position - #12

Oh My Goodness
Released 30th March 2012
Peak Chart Position - #13

Heart On My Sleeve
Released 4th March 2011
Peak Chart Position - #20

Hand On Heart
Released 22nd November 2013
Peak Chart Position - #25

Right Place Right Time
Released 23rd August 2013
Peak Chart Position - #27

Busy (EP)
Released 27th May 2011
Peak Chart Position - #45

ALBUMS

Right Place Right Time
Released 26th November 2012
Peak Chart Position - #1

In Case You Didn't Know
Released 25th November 2011
Peak Chart Position - #1

Olly Murs
Released 26th November 2010
Peak Chart Position - #2

He may have once dreamed of holding the FA Cup but although he's in another industry entirely, his trophy cabinet is not short of silverware. The award nominations just keep coming – most recently his nod for a prestigious Ivor Novello Songwriting Award. Deservedly so, we say!

TROPHY CABINET

BRIT AWARDS

2014 Nominated for British Single of the Year
Dear Darlin'

2013 Nominated for British Single of the Year
Trouble Maker

2013 Nominated for British Male Solo Artist
Himself

2012 Nominated for British Single of the Year
Heart Skips a Beat

2011 Nominated for British Single of the Year
Please Don't Let Me Go

IVOR NOVELLO AWARDS

2014 Nominated for Most Performed Work
Troublemaker

2013 Nominated for Most Performed Work
Dance with Me Tonight

MTV EUROPE MUSIC AWARDS

2013 Nominated for Best UK & Ireland Act
Himself

BBC RADIO 1 TEEN AWARDS

2013 Winner of Best British Solo Artist
Himself

2011 Winner of Best British Album
Olly Murs

NICKELODEON KIDS CHOICE AWARDS

2013 Nominated for Favourite UK
Male Artist
Himself

2012 Winner of Favourite UK
Male Artist
Himself

RADIO DISNEY MUSIC AWARDS

2014 Nominated for Best Song to
Dance to
Dance With Me Tonight

2013 Nominated for Best
Acoustic Performance
Heart Skips a Beat

2013 Nominated for Best Crush Song
Heart Skips a Beat

NORDOFF ROBBINS 02 SILVER CLEF AWARDS

2013 Nominated for Best Live Act
Himself

BT DIGITAL MUSIC AWARDS

2011 Winner of Best Male Artist
Himself

2011 Nominated for Best Newcomer
Himself

ROBBIE WILLIAMS

Olly has described Robbie as one of his best friends and the pair continue to collaborate. Their first duet was on The X Factor when they sang 'Angels', but since then they recorded 'I Wanna Be Like You' together and performed the track at The Royal Variety Show in 2013. Olly has also been special guest on Robbie's 'Take the Crown' stadium tour and Rob even cameoed in Olly's video for 'Hand On Heart' which is a homage to Robbie's 'Angels' video.

RIZZLE KICKS

Olly loved working with the British hip-hop duo. They featured on his hit track 'Heart Skips a Beat' which they performed to a great reception at The Brit Awards in 2012.

FLO RIDA

Olly and his co-writers envisaged working with Flo Rida on 'Troublemaker' from the outset but were concerned that, being the biggest rapper in the world, he may not be interested. They needn't have worried. From the moment he heard the track he was fully on board and wrote an awesome rap section for the track. The song was a huge success and received an Ivor Novello Songwriting nod.

CHIDDY BANG

Chiddy (Chidera Anamege, to use his full name) performed the rap section on the US version of Olly's hit song 'Heart Skips a Beat'. The Philadelphia based rapper is big news in the States and Olly loved working with him, shooting a new, soccer focused video.

COOL COLLABORATIONS

NIALL HORAN

Lovely Niall popped up in in a clip of Olly performing an acoustic version of 'Heart Skips a Beat'. The clip, shown on YouTube, shows Olly and his backing singers in full flow when the camera pans round to reveal Niall, sitting on the toilet, strumming his guitar. Niall then comes out and joins the group for the remainder of the track. Hilarious!

GARY BARLOW

Gary and Olly share a mutual respect for each other's talents. When Gary performed at the Royal Albert Hall in aid of The Prince's Trust in 2011, he asked Olly to take to the stage with him. The pair duetted on Take That hit 'Shine'.

Journalists just can't get enough of Mr Murs. Here are just a few of the more recent splashes that have appeared in the press. When you've finished reading, see if you can spot the red herring story which was not in the news.

Read All

1 Deal replacement!

Olly Murs set to 'freshen things up' on The X Factor... but this time as a JUDGE

TRUE ☐ FALSE ☐

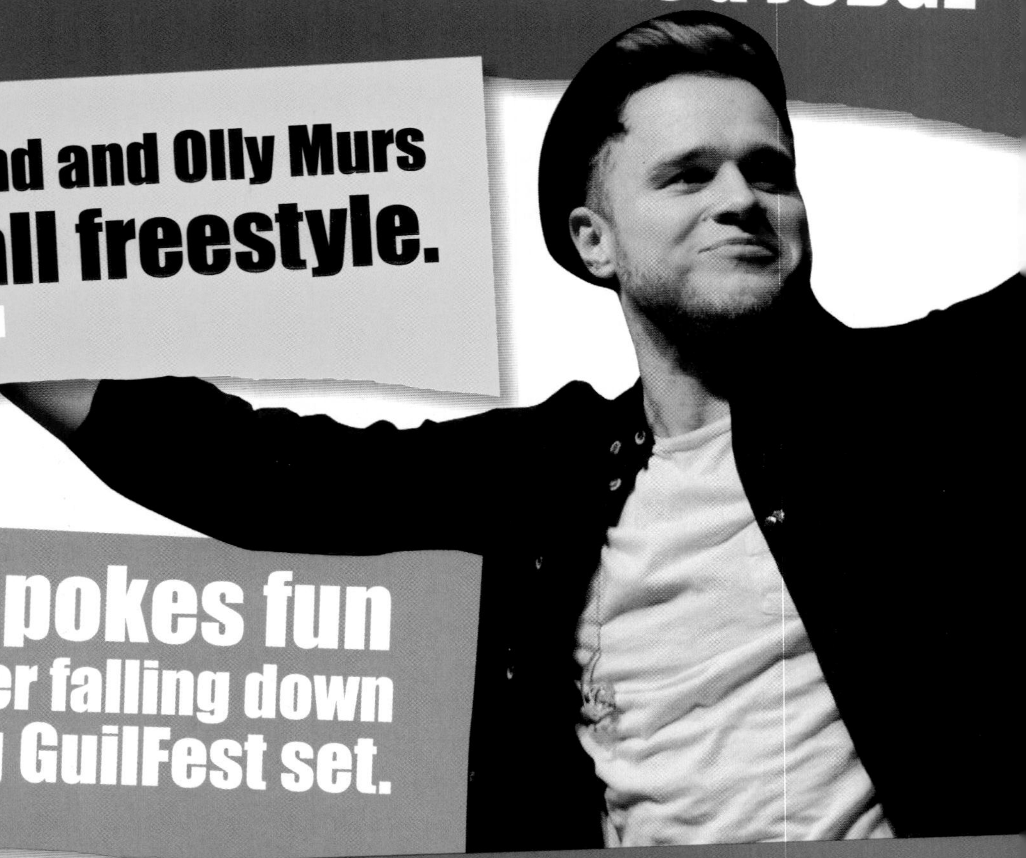

2 Rio Ferdinand and Olly Murs in football freestyle.

TRUE ☐ FALSE ☐

3 Olly Murs pokes fun at himself after falling down stairs during GuilFest set.

TRUE ☐ FALSE ☐

4 Murs pays £20,000 to go golfing with his Manchester United idols!

TRUE ☐ FALSE ☐

About HIM

5 Olly Murs presented with 'lordship' for his **30th birthday.**

TRUE ☐ FALSE ☐

6 **MURS-TERMIND – OLLY TO HOST** CELEBRITY-PACKED QUIZ.

TRUE ☐ FALSE ☐

7 Ron Bleurgh-gundy! Olly Murs copies Will Ferrell's Anchorman character... and admits he showered naked with the star.

TRUE ☐ FALSE ☐

8 He's just a big kid! Olly Murs swaps the hat for Mickey ears and dances with Goofy at Disneyland.

TRUE ☐ FALSE ☐

9 HE'S A TRAILBLAZER! CHARITY AMBASSADOR OLLY MURS IS SUITED AND BOOTED AS HE HEADLINES RAYS OF SUNSHINE EVENT

TRUE ☐ FALSE ☐

10 Who knew they were friends? Murs working with Kaiser Chief's drummer for new album.

TRUE ☐ FALSE ☐

BORN TO PERFORM

Olly knows exactly how to get a crowd jumping. Cast your eyes over this montage of the pop star busting his favourite moves. Each and every one is trademark Olly!

The Olly wiggle.

The cheeky twerk.

The flying scissor!

The tuck jump.

The wave of glory.

The high kick.

The 'your turn' point.

The Murs Army salute.

The 'lost in music'.

The 'two step'.

STYLE 'n'

In a sea of wannabes, try-hards and lookylikeys, Mister Murs stands out. Why? Because the guy has a unique style that's all his own – and he wears everything with confidence. Olly's style hasn't changed that much since The X Factor auditions - he still has his go-to Fred Perry pieces and pork-pie hats. As Olly's career has progressed though, so his fashion flair has developed and he's started pushing boundaries and taking clever risks. Read on to discover more about Olly's key looks.

SHOES

Olly loves Russell & Bromley shoes and wears them often. He's also a big fan of Chelsea boots "They're easy to slip on, work with different colours and you can wear them casual or really smart."

HATS

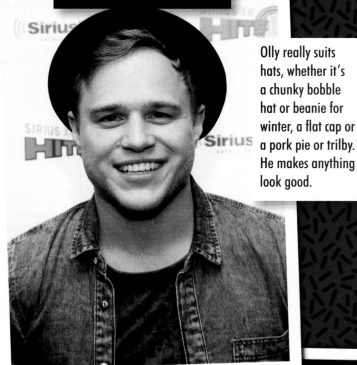

Olly really suits hats, whether it's a chunky bobble hat or beanie for winter, a flat cap or a pork pie or trilby. He makes anything look good.

CASUAL

When it comes to a more casual look, Olly loves denim, a snuggly jumper or a shirt with short, turned up sleeves!

SWAGGER

> "I've found what I love most about clothes, what works for me and what suits me."

WHISTLE & FLUTES

BLAZERS

Olly increasingly mixes High Street and designer pieces and loves blazers and jackets from labels like Margiela and Sandro.

Olly loves dressing up for major events and always looks dapper in a suit. He also rocks a waistcoat.

COLOUR

Olly's not afraid to give outfits a pop of colour, or wear eye-catching tones. He says, "I think everyone should be a bit more confident: if it's a summer's day, wear some bright colours. It's all about picking the right day and the right colours to suit it."

Olly AND THE IVY

Imagine you get the ultimate Christmas present – an entire day with Olly Murs all to yourself! Have you ever thought how you might spend those precious twenty-four hours? Close your eyes and allow yourself to dream up every detail of your day and then fill in your fabulous, fun-filled itinerary.

9AM ....

10AM ....

11AM ....

12PM ....

1PM ....

2PM ....

....

3PM ....

....

4PM ....

....

5PM ....

....

6PM ....

....

7PM ....

....

8PM ....

....

9PM ....

....

Aaaargh! Me 'n' Rob on The Big One at Blackpool Pleasure Beach.

Time to 'musk up' – me as Ron Burgundy at the Anchorman 2 premiere.

'Aving A

Did someone say swimming? Me and Grimmy off Radio 1.

Getting in the World Cup spirit!

Cooling an afro-clad Aston Merrygold off at Soccer Aid 2012.

Can I touch your 'fro? Being interviewed for the Tonight Show.

Laugh

Olly just loves larking around. The crazy Polaroids in this scrapbook prove that Olly's always up for a good giggle with his mates.

Sharing a joke with Caz in Brum for The X Factor.

Did someone say cake? Celebrating the No. 1 spot in style!

Olly Murs

31

Olly
Murs

The Kindred Spirit

Olly and Robbie Williams have masses in common. Besides their working class backgrounds and cheeky-chappy personas, they both have fantastic stage presence. In 2013 Robbie invited Olly to tour with him around the UK and Europe. On-stage, the chemistry was electric. Off-stage the boys bonded over their mutual love of football, with Olly becoming a constant fixture in Robbie's Soccer Aid teams.

The Presenting Partner

Olly and Caroline Flack created a fabulous on-screen partnership when they worked together on The Xtra Factor. The pair have since formed an enduring friendship. Olly was the first to congratulate Caroline on the launch of her new video show Viral Tap.

The Footie Friends

Olly has made some great friends through his enduring involvement with Soccer Aid. He loves hanging out with Danny Jones from McFly and comedians John Bishop and Jack Whitehall on and off the pitch. Danny and Olly amused themselves playing FIFA between Soccer Aid training sessions and Olly tweeted funny snaps of him and Jack Whitehall mucking about inside the Soccer Aid changing rooms.

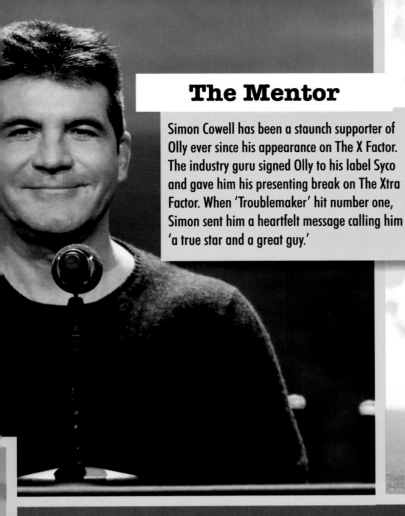

The Mentor

Simon Cowell has been a staunch supporter of Olly ever since his appearance on The X Factor. The industry guru signed Olly to his label Syco and gave him his presenting break on The Xtra Factor. When 'Troublemaker' hit number one, Simon sent him a heartfelt message calling him 'a true star and a great guy.'

The Band of Brothers

Olly has a close friendship with the boys from recently-split band JLS. Oritsé, Marvin, JB and Aston have supported Olly on his journey since day one. When Marvin married Rochelle Humes at Blenheim palace Olly was in attendance, even taking to the stage to perform some of the couple's fave songs.

The Pundit Pal

Former England international Rio Ferdinand and Olly have bonded over their love of the beautiful game. The pair were the perfect pick as presenters for the 'World Cup's 50 Greatest Moments' on BBC3.

When you're a great guy, you're bound to have lots of great mates! Take a peek inside Olly's address book and read about the artist's inner circle.

MURS' MATES

Here's Olly On...

... leaving The Xtra Factor

"I love the show, but I was very conscious that my music should come first. Also, when I do the job half-heartedly and am not around for auditions and boot camp, it's not fair on Caroline and the show itself. They deserve to have someone around on a more regular basis."

... stadium tours

"I would love to do a stadium tour. You have to be a certain artist to do it. Robbie has had the most amazing career over the past 20 years, so he has every right to do stadiums. One Direction - even though it's been a short career - the success of the guys and how big they are, it's going to be massive. I don't think I'm quite ready for it yet, but it's all about progression, and like every artist, I'll just dream and pray I'll get the opportunity."

... being in the studio

"I've been in the studio nearly every day. I'm working on the new album, and I'm really excited about people hearing it... We're jamming and trying new ideas and new styles, doing something you haven't quite done before, yet keeping it generic, keeping it pop and quite fun. We go in with an open mind and try to come up with a hit - just a really good song."

... dating

"Always go to a restaurant on the first date, so you can get to know them. You can have a good chat. The second date should always be an activity... It's about having fun. Dating is fun. It's exciting!"

... the haters

"There's always going to be someone out there who doesn't like what you do, doesn't like your style, your face. That's part of life. But I feed off that. I don't think I'd be where I am today if it wasn't for that. It puts a little fire in the belly, keeps me going so I can prove so many people wrong."

... his music

"My music is fun, happy, never depressing, I don't like to make people cry, I like to make them smile and have a good day. I want people to have a good time, that's always been my aim."

... success

"I think what makes a successful man is just determination and kind of knowing who you are and where you want to go to and having that ambition. I've been successful and I'm proud to have that and no one can take that away from me. I think in any job you can get there through hard work and determination…if you want to be a bank manager you can strive to be a bank manager. It's about achievement - everyone has something to be proud of at some point in their life."

... gaming

"I love video games. I've got a PS4 at home. At the moment I'm playing Tomb Raider and FIFA… If there was a game about a musical career or something, I might be interested in contributing. I'm surprised The X Factor haven't done something like that."

... The Brits

"You go there and it's just good to be in a room with loads of different artists you haven't seen for a while. I mean it's obviously very difficult when you lose - you don't like to lose, but it is good to catch up with everyone and have a giggle."

BEST FOOT FORWARD

As a youngster, Olly's talent saw him play semi-professionally for local side Witham FC. His dreams of playing in the premier league were scuppered by an injury, but the raw talent and enthusiasm remain.

MAN CRUSH!

Olly's not afraid to admit his love for key players. "I had all Giggsy's pictures up on my wall and had Giggs' name on the back of my shirt as well. Then obviously Becks – I was a massive Beckham fan as a kid – I had the blonde hair, the Predators, I thought I was him!"

UNITED WE STAND

Olly is a die-hard Manchester United Fan and as a season ticket holder, he tries to make at least six home games a year. His choice of team might seem strange but Olly had his reasons: "I've never been someone to follow the crowd and it would've been easy for me to pick a London team but at the time I just didn't think they were the teams for me. My Dad was a United fan and was always trying to convince me to be so I decided they'd be my team. Everyone at school caned me for it but when Beckham came along that's when I knew it was alright… Even today people say I'm a Cockney Red but I'm used to it – like water off a duck's back!"

SING WHEN YOU'RE WINNING

Olly considered recording a World Cup theme for Rio 2014. He said, "If I was to do it I would like to do it with someone else, make it a cool collaboration, maybe I could speak to Rizzle Kicks and do something with them?"

GIVING BACK

Olly often has the opportunity to get involved in charity football matches. He regularly takes part in the celebrity football tournament Soccer Six and has played three times for the Soccer Aid England team organized by pal Robbie Williams, raising huge amounts of money for UNICEF. In January 2013, Olly was appointed an ambassador for the Football Association – a role which connects him at grass roots level, showing kids that anyone can get involved with football. As part of the FA's 150th anniversary celebrations, Olly and Radio 1 presenter Nick Grimshaw put together two teams to slog it out at St George's Park and Wembley. Olly's team was twice triumphant – winning 11-1 and clinching the other on penalties after a 3-3 draw.

A PITCH

If you're not a footie fan you may be just about to turn this page, but don't just yet. If he's not playing, he's watching or tweeting about it and the generous lad takes part in many charity matches to raise money for fantastic causes such as Soccer Aid and Soccer Six! So be inspired by his passion and let Olly share some of his football fever…

41

1. I'll soon be able to crack nuts @ gpwhyte after those sumo squats this morning!! The old _____ _____ is in bits!!

2. Just took seat @ Wimbledon men's finals!! I'm backing _____!!!

3. Great fun @RoyalAlbertHall @ RaysofSunshine gig!! Love this charity!! Such a _____ forgetting the _____ haha thanks for helping me out lol

4. Couple of cold BBQ _____ for breakfast!! #LivingTheDream

5. Ledge day working with this guy @ rioferdy5 can't tell you what yet But proper _____!!

6. Watching GIGGSYs press conference! buzzing! Old Trafford will be rocking Sat! ____ __ _____? Definitely the Biggest decision for him

7. So _____ today.. Troublemaker has been nominated at @BASCA_UK #TheIvors PRS for Music Most Performed Work. So delighted!! ACE!!!! X

8. Easter Sunday game time playing the legendary POP-UP PIRAAT with This _____ _____!!

ALL OF A TWITTER

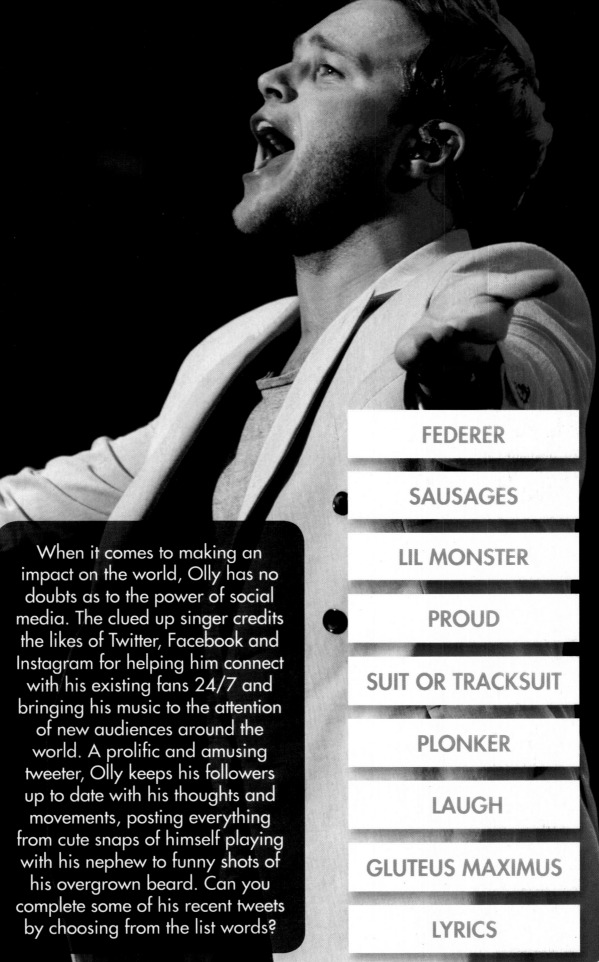

When it comes to making an impact on the world, Olly has no doubts as to the power of social media. The clued up singer credits the likes of Twitter, Facebook and Instagram for helping him connect with his existing fans 24/7 and bringing his music to the attention of new audiences around the world. A prolific and amusing tweeter, Olly keeps his followers up to date with his thoughts and movements, posting everything from cute snaps of himself playing with his nephew to funny shots of his overgrown beard. Can you complete some of his recent tweets by choosing from the list words?

FEDERER

SAUSAGES

LIL MONSTER

PROUD

SUIT OR TRACKSUIT

PLONKER

LAUGH

GLUTEUS MAXIMUS

LYRICS

CELEBRITY JUICE

Keith Lemon is a big fan of the Murs and has asked him on his very funny ITV2 show many times. Olly has acquitted himself well in the face of extreme mickey-taking despite finding himself getting asked to take his shirt off, pucker up to Keith and talk about his dating history.

GRAHAM NORTON SHOW

Olly appeared on the hit chat show in March 2013 to perform and promote his new single Army of Two. After a fantastic performance he was called to the sofa alongside Hollywood royalty, Jude Law, Dame Judy Dench and Mila Kunis whereupon Graham outed his celebrity crush… on Mila. 'I didn't think in my wildest dreams I'd ever meet her!' Olly cried.

THE X FACTOR

Olly has returned on several occasions to the series that launched his career. In 2013 he performed 'Hand On Heart' to a fantastic reception from the studio audiences and was also invited out to New York to be a guest judge with Gary Barlow at Judges' Houses.

AS SEEN

ROYAL VARIETY PERFORMANCE

After his performance with special guest Robbie Williams, Olly was thrilled to meet His Royal Highness Prince Charles and Camilla Duchess of Cornwall, when he performed at The Royal Variety Show in London in November 2013. Olly was in his smartest attire when he shook hands with the prince after performing to the delighted audience at the Palladium theatre.

THE TONIGHT SHOW

While in America, Olly did the rounds of some of the biggest TV shows including Dancing With The Stars, Good Morning America and The View. He was even invited to appear on America's flagship talk and entertainment show The Tonight Show. He made a big impression on each and every show, performing in the studio and chatting and joking with big name hosts including the legendary Jay Leno.

Whether he's performing, presenting or appearing as a super, smashing special guest, Olly has been on our screens for the last five years! Having started out on one of the biggest shows on the planet, he's right at home in front of the camera. Take a look at some of his most famous appearances.

ON SCREEN

MAKE-IT:

FRINGED FAN TEE

GOT A COOL OLLY T-SHIRT? WHY NOT HAVE A GO AT MAKING YOURS UNIQUE?

YOU WILL NEED:
- One Olly Murs T-shirt
- Scissors
- Beads (optional)

CLOTHES DON'T COME CHEAP! ALWAYS CHECK WITH AN ADULT BEFORE YOU START CUSTOMISING.

WHAT TO DO:

1. Lay your T-shirt out flat on a clean work surface.
2. Cut off the collar to make a wider neckline. Now cut off the sleeves to make the tee into a vest shape. Pull on the fabric around these edges to make them look less 'new'.
3. Starting a couple of centimetres off to one side, cut from the bottom hem upwards to just under the bust line or just below the print on the front. Cut another strip a little away along from this, then continue snipping strips all the way around. These strips will become your fringing.
4. Turn the T-shirt over and repeat the fringe on the back.
5. Take each string of the fringe, then give it a good pull and a twist. Move your way round the top, working on each one. By the end your fringing should look grungy and rope-like.
6. Now thread a bead on to the bottom of each string and secure with it a knot. If you'd rather not use beads you can just tie knots instead.

WISH OLLY COULD BE BY YOUR SIDE, ALWAYS? WELL NOW HE CAN! THIS CUTE TOTE BAG IS GREAT FOR THE BEACH, THE PARK OR THE MALL. THE BONUS IS THAT IT'S ALSO SUPER-EASY TO MAKE – NO SEWING REQUIRED!

YOU WILL NEED:

- One plain T-shirt (the bigger the tee, the bigger the bag!)
- Marker pen
- Ruler
- Scissors
- Duct tape (if you can get it in a bright colour this will look great, but black is also fine)
- Staple gun
- Fabric pens

WHAT YOU DO:

1. Lay your T-shirt out flat on a clean work surface.
2. Your first job is to make the garment look like a V-neck vest. Make a mark five centimetres under the sleeve at the edge of the tee and then five centimetres across towards the centre. Join the two dots with a line.
3. Take your ruler and draw a line from the inner end of the line up to the halfway point of the top seam. Repeat on the other side.
4. Mark out a V on the neckline and cut along those lines. Your T-shirt should now look like a vest! Turn it inside out and spread it out flat so there are no lumps or wrinkles.
5. It's time to create the waterproof lining for the bag. Start at the bottom hem of the tee and cover it with a strip of duct tape, then work your way up laying strips of duck tape until the T-shirt is completely covered. Fold the ends around to the other side. Flip the tee over and repeat this. You will end up with what looks like a plastic tank top!
6. With your ruler, make a mark five centimetres up from the bottom at one edge of the tee, then do the same at the other edge. Join the marks to make a horizontal line running all the way across the bottom. Flip the bag over and repeat this on the other side.
7. Now put your hands inside the tee and rotate it a quarter of the way round so it looks more like a bag shape. The straps of your vest have now become bag handles!
8. Take your stapler and staple all the way along the black line you've drawn. Make sure the staples are close together otherwise things will fall out of the bottom.
9. Now grab your scissors and cut a slit at the edges from the bottom up to the staple. Repeat this on the other side. Fold the bottom flap up and secure it with more tape.
10. Your bag is nearly ready. Turn it inside out and use fabric pens to decorate it with Murs graffiti!

TEE TOTE-A-LLY OLLY!

THE JOURNEY

"I'm really proud of my fans. It's been a slow journey for us really. It started when I came off The X Factor. I felt everyone doubted me but the reason I was able to come back with a bang was because of the fans. It's just grown really the past 2 years, and I hope people will continue to like me. I want to grow with my fans like Robbie Williams did."

OLIVER'S ARMY

TATTS CRAZY

"Some of my fans have tattoos of me. I don't get freaked out by it. It's obviously very flattering for them to get lyrics on their arms. But I think to get my picture or Olly Murs is a bit much… only because when they get married their husband's going to be like 'why do you have Olly Murs on your bum?'"

BLOGGERS

"I often visit fan sites, there are quite a few blogs and sites that people put online. I really appreciate it all. Those guys are so on it and actually get stuff up before we do, so if I say, do a gig in Austria and there's a video link, they'll have it already online, it's great."

YOUR SONG

"Army of Two was written for my Murs Army. It's a hard thing to do, to write for the fans without sounding naff, but I wanted to write something for my fans who have been amazing to me."

IF YOU HAVEN'T YET JOINED THE MURS ARMY, THEN WHAT HAVE YOU BEEN WAITING FOR? OLLY'S VERY APPRECIATIVE OF HIS FANS AND ALWAYS TAKES TIME TO MEET AND GREET THEM. CAN YOU SPOT YOURSELF IN THESE FAN PHOTOS?

SHOWBIZ FAN

"I did a gig in Glasgow and my tour manager said, 'Susan Boyle's at the box office.' We didn't have any free tickets left for the show and they apologised. She said, "that's fine, I've come to buy tickets." She came backstage afterwards. We got a picture together and she was very complimentary. She's such a nice person. We had a chat and she said she liked what I did and I thought, 'Susan Boyle is standing here saying she likes my stuff and she's sold 12 million records.' It was surreal."

It's A Mad Murs World

WANT TO EARN SUPER FAN STATUS IN THE MURS ARMY? HERE ARE SOME IDEAS TO HELP YOU DO JUST THAT...

Be generous

Olly always does his bit for charity. Take a leaf out of the generous guy's book and hold a fun event to raise money for a good cause. You could hold a football tournament, a bake sale or a disco dance-a-thon to Olly's tunes. Pick a charity Olly holds dear, such as Sport Relief or Brainwave or find another equally deserving cause.

Make your own lyric video

Olly has released some awesome lyric videos. Remember the graphic shapes of 'Oh My Goodness' and the fun montage of shots featured in 'Dance With Me Tonight'? Now have a go yourself. Grab a tablet, mobile or hand-held video camera and get filming. Check out OllyMursVEVO for inspiration.

Q & A

Ever thought of holding an Olly quiz night? Assemble your stats and facts and invite fellow fans to come round and test their knowledge. You could award Olly-related prizes to the winners.

Fan fiction

The trend for fan fiction and self-publishing is huge right now. Why not pick up a pen and try penning your own Olly-centred story. You could put yourself in the novel or create a set of totally new characters to come into contact with Olly.

Photo opportunity

Olly loves a celebrity selfie – just check out his Twitter feed. If you haven't already captured the great man on film, make it your mission to get a real-life photo with Olly. Check out his website for news of his latest gigs and appearances and see if you can snap the ultimate shot.

Try decoupage

Give a beloved item a Murs-over. Decoupage involves using cuttings to cover something like a book, a box or even an item of furniture. You'll need to assemble a collection of your favourite magazine cuttings and pictures of Olly, or scraps of material from Olly merchandise to get started. You'll need enough so that when laid on and slightly overlapping they cover the item entirely. Then just buy some decoupage glue from a craft shop and get sticking.

Un-convention-al

Why not hold an Olly Murs fan convention? You could start small at your house and then move to a bigger venue nearby as word spreads. Get together, put Olly's latest album on and share your love of Mr Murs.

Start your own blog

Olly has a blog on his official website where he shares all his latest news with his fans. After checking out the latest from Olly, think about charting your own personal fan journey in your own blog.

TALK LIKE A LOCAL

Your guide to the kind of Essex-isms you may have heard Olly utter.

Ledge!	Abbrieviation of the word legendary. Meaning awesome or fantastic.
Proper	Meaning 'very', or used to describe something done really well ie "Man U gave Everton a proper thrashing."
Mint	Brilliant.
Oh my god!	Crikey!
Shut up!	I'm very surprised by that.
Sweet as!	That's great.
Pukka	Brilliant.

STRANGE BUT TRUE ESSEX FACTS...

1. Danbury Common hosts the largest population of Adders (venomous snakes) in the UK.

2. Ashingdon village is the sunniest place in the UK.

3. People living in Essex are 38% more likely to be hit by falling aeroplane parts, than anywhere else in Britain.

4. In 1701 a man called Richard Bradley introduced the first crocodile into the UK. He kept it in the lake of his home in Braintree, Essex.

Hometown

They say 'you can take the boy out of Essex, but you'll never take Essex out of the boy,' and Olly is an Essex lad born and bred. Here's all you need to know about the county Olly's proud to call home.

FAMOUS ESSEX-ONIANS

Olly isn't the only talent to come out of this county. It's a who's who of the great and good including these A-listers…

Michelle Dockery – Actress – Downtown Abbey

Russell Brand – Comedian and author

Maggie Smith – Actress

Jessie J – Singer/Songwriter

Rochelle Humes & Frankie Sandford – singers – The Saturdays

Dermot O'Leary – Presenter

Jamie Oliver – Chef

Rupert Grint – Actor

Anya Hindmarch – Designer

Nick Frost – Actor

John Constable – Landscape Painter

William Gilberd – Chief Physician to Queen Elizabeth 1 and scientist. Discovered the earth's magnetism.

County Your Blessings

Essex is a coastal county in the East of England, bordered by Cambridgeshire and Suffolk to the North, Hertfordshire to the West, London to the South West, and Kent to the South. It measures 1300 square miles. The county town of Essex is Chelmsford. Large parts of Essex are rural, but it also has bustling market towns and the longest coastline of any English county with traditional English seaside resorts like Southend-On-Sea and stunning Blue Flag beaches such as Chalkwell Beach and Martelllo Bay.

30 Reasons To Love Olly Murs

1 He's humble in the face of royalty.

2 Robbie Williams is in his phone book...

3 ... as is Gary Barlow.

4 He's not afraid to take the mick out of himself.

5 He loves his family.

6 He can bust a move – seriously! Michael Bublé even asked him to teach him to dance.

7 He loves a selfie!

8 He loves a cuddle with a huge foam character.

9 He'll climb mountains – or at least scale railings – to meet his fans.

10 He's an old fashioned, chivalrous gent.

11 He can play air guitar...

12 ...and the real thing.

13 He looks hot in headgear.

14 He loves dogs.

15 He loves kids.

Olly has officially waved goodbye to his twenties after hitting the big 3 – 0 on May 14th 2014. Here are 30 reasons we'll still adore him even when he's 90 and walking around with a zimmer frame!

16 He can actually sing... live.

17 He always looks like he's having fun.

18 His teeth are whiter than snow.

19 He can fly.

20 He's happy to open up about his love life and admits to being terrified of ending up alone.

21 He sometimes goes 'out there' with the footwear.

22 He's always up for a snog.

23 He likes a good old cuppa.

24 He loves football.

25 He's a great sportsman.

26 He shops!

27 He does his bit for charity.

28 He's a consummate showman.

29 He's met Kermit the Frog.

30 He's just gorgeous.

MAKE-IT:
LOVELY LYRIC POSTER

Want to vamp up a dull wall in your bedroom or den? Well, why not Olly-fy it with this cool craft idea?

You Will Need:

- An old picture frame
- A large sheet of paper or card the same size as or bigger than your frame
- Coloured pens
- An alphabet stencil (optional)
- The lyrics to your favourite Olly Murs track

What To Do:

1. Cut the paper to fit the size of the frame.
2. Find a portion of the lyrics you love most.
3. Arrange them in different fonts on the paper. You could use different font styles and colours.
4. Fix your lyric poster inside your frame.
5. Hang the frame on the wall.

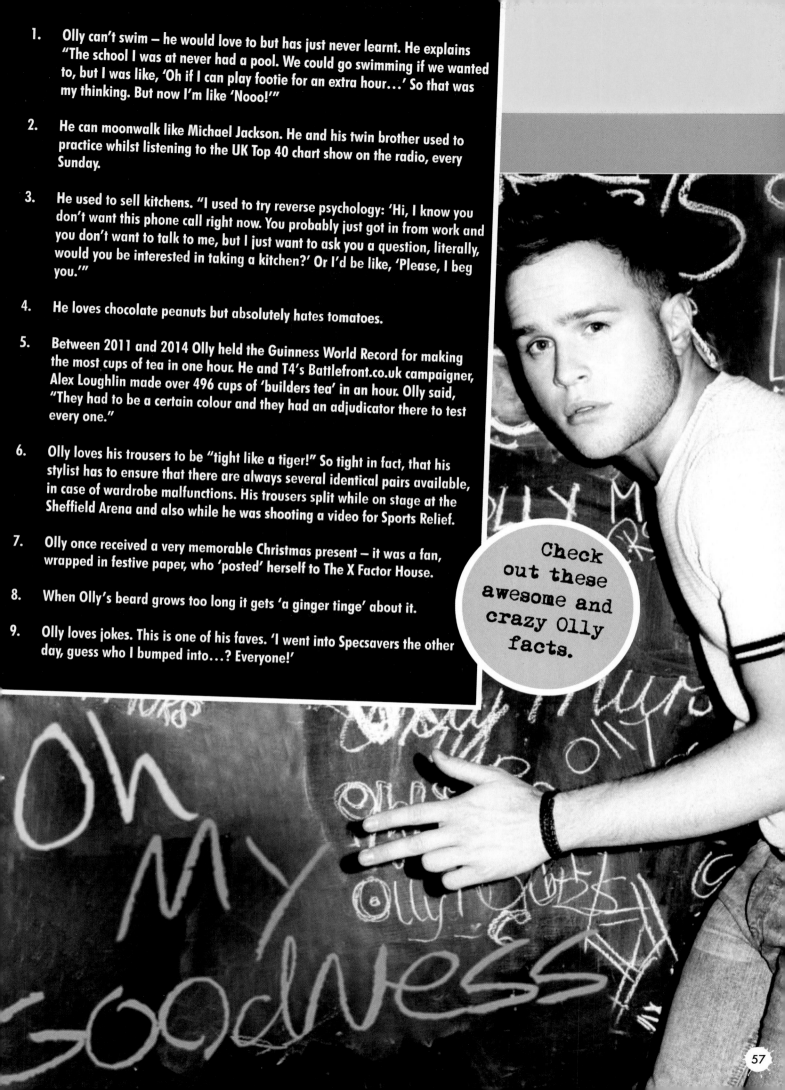

1. Olly can't swim – he would love to but has just never learnt. He explains "The school I was at never had a pool. We could go swimming if we wanted to, but I was like, 'Oh if I can play footie for an extra hour…' So that was my thinking. But now I'm like 'Nooo!'"

2. He can moonwalk like Michael Jackson. He and his twin brother used to practice whilst listening to the UK Top 40 chart show on the radio, every Sunday.

3. He used to sell kitchens. "I used to try reverse psychology: 'Hi, I know you don't want this phone call right now. You probably just got in from work and you don't want to talk to me, but I just want to ask you a question, literally, would you be interested in taking a kitchen?' Or I'd be like, 'Please, I beg you.'"

4. He loves chocolate peanuts but absolutely hates tomatoes.

5. Between 2011 and 2014 Olly held the Guinness World Record for making the most cups of tea in one hour. He and T4's Battlefront.co.uk campaigner, Alex Loughlin made over 496 cups of 'builders tea' in an hour. Olly said, "They had to be a certain colour and they had an adjudicator there to test every one."

6. Olly loves his trousers to be "tight like a tiger!" So tight in fact, that his stylist has to ensure that there are always several identical pairs available, in case of wardrobe malfunctions. His trousers split while on stage at the Sheffield Arena and also while he was shooting a video for Sports Relief.

7. Olly once received a very memorable Christmas present – it was a fan, wrapped in festive paper, who 'posted' herself to The X Factor House.

8. When Olly's beard grows too long it gets 'a ginger tinge' about it.

9. Olly loves jokes. This is one of his faves. 'I went into Specsavers the other day, guess who I bumped into…? Everyone!'

Check out these awesome and crazy Olly facts.

revealed his celebrity crush live on air. It was Mila Kunis – who was also on the show.

B **is for Barcelona FC**
Massive footy fan Olly visited the ground and had pics taken with the players.

C **is for Calico Cat Café**
Olly visited this crazy joint while in Japan. He described it as 'a bunch of cats cruising around while you're having a drink.' Random!

D **is for Deal or No Deal**
Not Olly's game. Enough said!

E **is for Essex**
(where else!)

F **is for Flirty 30s**
Since his 30th birthday Olly's now a paid up member of this club.

we love it when the boy flashes his gnashers.

H **is for Happy Days**
Olly's illustrated autobiography.

I **is for Ivor Novello**
Olly was thrilled to be nominated for this prestigious song-writing award for Troublemaker.

J **is for Jam**
The Jam. Olly is a big fan and has covered Town Called Malice in his live gigs.

K **is for Keith Lemon**
The naughty northerner made Olly remove his hat for a cheeky kiss on Celebrity Juice.

L **is for Latvia**
Olly has an exotic European heritage. His paternal grandparents were Latvian.

A B C D E F G H I J K L

M **is for Mothers**
Olly gave fans a chance to win personal video messages for their special mums on Mother's Day!

N **is for Nuts**
His favourites are peanuts.

O **is for Owner**
Olly finally owns his own home, having lived with his parents in Witham for years.

P **is for Pig**
Olly puckered up to Miss Piggy.

Q **is for Quirky**
He's one of a kind alright!

R **is for Rhythmic Gymnastics**
yes, ribbons, hoops and balls. Olly tried his hand for Sport Relief.

S **is for Studio**
Olly works hard in the studio, writing songs for his albums.

T **is for Twitter**
5.7million followers and counting.

U **is for USA**
Olly's enjoying huge success over the pond and has performed live on shows like Dancing with the Stars and Good Morning America.

V **is for Vintage**
Olly loves to mix finds from vintage stores, with high street and designer pieces.

W **is for Witham**
Olly's hometown.

X **is for X Factor**
Where it all began!

Y **is for You!**
Fans like you are at the heart of everything Olly does.

Z **is for Zoos**
Olly loves a zoo and while touring the world often spends some down time checking out the animals. He visited Taronga Zoo in Sydney and more recently the Tokyo Zoo in Japan.

An A – Z Of Olly

'A he's adorable, B he's so beautiful, C he's a chirpy, cheeky guy…' Get to know the man inside out, back to front and alphabetically with this fun list.

To all my fans!
See you soon,
much love xx

ANSWERS

PAGE 14

1. d)
2. e)
3. a)
4. c)
5. b)

PAGES 20 - 21

All are true apart from number 6. Olly has not announced plans to host Mastermind.

PAGES 41-42

1. I'll soon be able to crack nuts @gpwhyte after those sumo squats this morning!! The old GLUTEUS MAXIMUS is in bits!!

2. Just took seat @ Wimbledon men's finals!! I'm backing FEDERER!!

3. Great fun @RoyalAlbertHall @RaysofSunshine gig!! Love this charity!! Such a PLONKER forgetting the LYRICS haha thanks for helping me out lol

4. Couple of cold BBQ SAUSAGES for breakfast!! #LivingTheDream

5. Ledge day working with this guy @rioferdy5 can't tell you what yet But proper LAUGH!!

6. Watching GIGGSYs press conference! buzzing! Old Trafford will be rocking Sat! SUIT OR TRACKSUIT Definitely the Biggest decision for him

7. So PROUD today.. Troublemaker has been nominated at @BASCA_UK #TheIvors PRS for Music Most Performed Work. So delighted!! ACE!!!! X

8. Easter Sunday game time playing the legendary POP-UP PIRAAT with This LIL MONSTER